i am not myself

To Clara,

Thank you for your support.
I pray this touches you.

God bless,

[signature]

Michael A. Campbell

Sunesis Ministries Ltd

Published by Sunesis Ministries Ltd. For more information about Sunesis Ministries Ltd, please visit:

www.stuartpattico.com

ISBN: 978-0-9930065-7-9

To The Chief Musician

family & friends

When I am masked, I am not myself
AFRICAN PROVERB
{extract taken from the book African Masks: from the
Barbier-Mueller Collection}

He had to wear it for years. And when he took
it off he found his own face had grown to fit
it. He was now really beautiful. What had
begun as disguise had become a reality.

C.S.LEWIS.

****

Contents

ACKNOWLEDGEMENTS 9

Wanting...12

Unpacking...15

Cradling her in my eyes...17

The Kitchen Altar 19

Gentleman's sport 20

3 Denials...22

Kumina 24

Dust...26

Weightlifters' Belt..28

Butterfly 30

Pulpit Calypso 32

Cussin' 37

Graffiti 39

Catching Brent 40

Mister Nobody..41

Box man 43

Reggae (island longing)...45

One Jamaica Morning 47

In the cool of its shade..54

Elephant dance 56

Coming to Come 58

ACKNOWLEDGEMENTS

i am not myself is a past-down wisdom. It predates this book and will no doubt survive this book. It is first and foremost a West African proverb that i saw in the introduction to the Barbier-Mueller collection of African masks. It would be short-sighted not to be aware of the politics behind the foreign archiving of African artefacts, but that is not on trial, neither is it central here. The African adage in its entirety reads: *'when I am masked, I am not myself'*. In the West, masks often connote hiddenness, or concealment. When someone is said to be wearing a mask, we would say that they have something to hide, that the person on display is not presenting us with who they really are. To some West African cultures of the past, the individual wearing the mask takes on another identity and this according to some is not a human being. The mask i am thinking about is reconstructive, it is the healer of the countenance that lies underneath. As C.S. Lewis has pointed out in *Mere Christianity*, if i wear this mask for a long period of time, i would find my 'face had grown to fit it, [that i was] now really beautiful.' The poems in this book are all true, once we establish that literature of this kind, is a well-meaning fiction of the facts. It is difficult to capture moments of true revelation, to transcribe experience to script. As carriers of meaning words do have their limits. With that being said, this could be interpreted as auto-biography. Some poems try to capture the beauty of sacrificial love, some the love of country, whether that be England or the West-Indies, others the love of God. All I hope is that the poems have succeeded in highlighting the virtues and experiences that

9

I believe has helped shape the face beneath the mask i now endeavoured to wear. Firstly, praise to the *Chief Musician*, the author and finisher of this orchestral arrangement, this life. I would also like to thank a secret benefactor who believed in the art so much, as to pay for and introduce me to a writing coach, please know that 'Mikey-dreadd', the name you so affectionately call me, appreciates everything. I must thank 'the storyteller' Eli Anderson for introducing me to experimentation, to stepping outside of the box into the unknown where poetry and poetic forms are concerned. Thanks to Mrs Rebecca Lindsay Campbell, Dervan Delroy Campbell, Kurt and Jerome for being family and at all times family. Thanks to Bishop Joe Aldred, Tracey Marquis, Christalina Fernandez, Karla Williams and Melonie McLeod for their readings of and responses to either the first, second or umpteenth draft of this book. Thanks to Angela Clarke and Jacqui Manning, two of the many spiritual mothers i am so blessed to have, not only for their support, but also their polite urgings. Finally, thanks to all my extended family and friends. i am not myself, i am also other people.

i
am
not
myself
POEMS

Wanting

i
want
to be playing
like
thinking

to be
thinking
to be something
in
feeling

i
want
to be feeling
like
knowing

to be
knowing
to be something
in
loving

i
want
to be loving
like
searching

to be
searching
to be something
in
healing

i
want
to be healing
like
loosing

to be
loosing
to be something
in
freeing

i
want
to be freeing
like
laughing

to be
laughing
to be something
in
weeping

i
want

to be weeping
like
praising

to be
praising
to be something
in
giving

i
want
to be giving
in
yielding

to be
yielding
to be something
in
blessing

Unpacking

i've decided to move out of my boxes
organise the library
get the hands dirty with the last several months
there's always the dust
to remind me of
the way of things.

Some books i've read
the others
untouched
and paper bags
brand names mostly
torn up. Binned.

Moths appear lodged
between denim
and shirts stale with sepia
snuffed under
the weight of their appetite
and in the corners of the room
the long-legs are strung up
good.

Then there's the shelved notes
dead sentiment left to ferment
drown and drunk me.
i always intend to throw them away
I don't.

i then found a Bible I'd lost

covered in 5 'o' clock shadow
unrecognisable in the dust
and the voices of my mind,
the wilderness in there
cries out

and i smile tears at my own repentance.

Cradling her in my eyes

To R. C.

The old photograph has you in a wedding dress
styling a Three-Piece shabine[1] that styles a side-
parted afro
behind red bougainvillea. Black is in style and
it's the 80s. The moment stretches prostrate,
and the photographer caught your veil slayed in the
Spirit,

still, a marriage pinned to celluloid is some life
sentence
even for a woman whose faith is working out its
permanence,
but those no-souls, with stiff smiles; a festoon on a
headstone,
live back in Jamaica's 85' springtime, embalmed in a
keepsake.—
Gone now is the marrow from the bone, the memory,
a vagabond,

walks to and fro outside the mind's four walls. In the
blink of aperture
you were changed, had to, couldn't be explained by
no glass eye,

---

[1] **Shabine:** Patois for an individual of afro-Caribbean descent
with fair complexion. This could be somebody of mixed heritage
or a mixed race. This is briefly explained in Derek Walcott's
'*Schooner Flight.*'

no rule of thirds could pin you down, no Golden mean
could sum you up. Like African art you collapsed the rules of
representation, into the foreign-familiar, primitive-sophisticated

carrying the gourd body of The Great Mother, draping over bone
rolls of time and contour. Your body is a map. The terrain tells of
how you gave up your belly for my brother and me, the silvers,
of a black lustre oxidised by life. Your eyes are yellow moons,
great mother-of-pearls to dupe your body's natives.

i, was the first settler to arrive and now i watch you on the walk of a quiet life.
My crescent eyes are on you, with a longing as felt as the trailing moon.
Believe when i say, i pray, that our time, will last longer than divine will.
i pray, that whatever i am to you is a benediction.
So i continue to bruise my knees.

The Kitchen Altar

Her pot sends up an incense of onion,
And smoke billows from the burning censer
Filling the atmosphere with praise. Not on
The hob, but by the stove is the altar

And the train of an old Banner Hymn sweeps
Throughout the kitchen making thick the space.
During the times when things were tough, she keeps
To spirituals — secrets had their place

In her *songs of freedom*, but were not kept
Secret when she sang them. We all knew when
Things were bad, onions were cut to cloves, left
On the fire to be baptised by it, then

She'd tongue something over the sizzling sound
Of rushing wind, some Pentecostal hum
Over the troubled cooking oil, that seemed
To lift the meal till God's presence done come.

Gentleman's sport

'I've never been stopped,'
he says shadowboxing.—
he skips in, whips the jab
steps out, then we both get stuck in,
we've got mid-air winded.
Blow by blow
we beat the bloat out its belly
use the paunch of the room as punchbag,
till the air is punch-drunk and wobbly
in front of the old radiant gas fire.

We are pigeon-toed
hunched with a raised guard
circling our opponent
in a crab then cross-armed-peek-a-boo.
And we dance together like this
for what was all night.

i hear how he stops the likes of White, Lagan, Dermit,
Lock.
How *'White went out like a light,'*
'Lagan out on points,'
'Dermit, right hook,'
'Lock's bout was a bloodbath…
… I felt on top of the world,' he whispers,
so as not to let my mother hear.

She howls freely, in a loud West Indian way,
about how he'd won a tonne

of trophies, a glass bowl, a clock, a couple of
transistor radios,
and how silly he was to give them all up.
He just shrugs his shoulders and says,
'It's a mug's game.'

After 16 fights, with no stoppages
he got stopped.
got hitched,
got saved, sanctified and filled with the Holy Spirit.

He's no mug.

3 Denials

The first time
was after he'd packed in his job.
He'd drive—
searching side roads
for what people
ate and left.
Stocking the van with
headboards,
warped slats,
spring mattress frames
eaten to the rust,
to weigh-in and trade for cash-in-hand.
"i swear, I dunno the man."

The second time
scrap was strewn out front
and back.
A sink, leant against the side of the shed,
Second-hand furniture splayed
by rubbish bins,
and he must've been bearded grisly
in his mind—
on his working-class hustle,
in a neighbourhood,
over on the middle-class side.

The third time
i saw him haul some new-old thing
onto the back of the boot,
what could've been:

a stove, washer-drier, fridge—
something big; headed straight for the yard.
He, a complete write-off to public opinion
thought nothing of it,
"i'm saying, I dunno the man!"

At night, we ate supper.
The muck-up was if nothing else, honest.
The scrap-work paid for the caked clods of rice,
the baked beans, the corn-beef hash.
He took pride in the fact
We'd eaten and were full.

In two weeks,
hard at the old calling again
he let a long electric fan ride up front,
pots and pans occupied passenger seats
the rest of the vehicle was stacked to the roof
with the same scrap metal.

Kumina[2]

In memory of Laurel Lewis

And kumina started as prayer
Meeting ended.
The yard around her home
Was a stamper hollowed-out.
In her absence they danced
Roundabout her memory,
& the *Kbandu*
Kept time-*time*.

My cousin's spliff between
Friends
Burned down to the very last
Wisp of soul.
To the point the marijuana
Ate out the stomach,
Did nothing for the heart.

In all that time nothing changed.
The dance didn't move my cousin's
Friends beyond frenzy.
Is just their t-shirts were damp
With sweat when the *Kbandu* again
Called time-*time*.

---

[2] **Kumina:** Kumina is a traditional Jamaican folk form involving dance, music and religious practices and beliefs. Kumina plays are primarily performed for funerals and memorials. The focus at all times is the invoking of ancestral spirits.

Social mourners slunk
Back-a-yard with nothing doing now,
Professional mourners hummed
Empty dirges through the funk
The Dead-yard drunk on weed smoke
Blasphemed Mama's God;
Mutilated the faith of that house.

Is better they'd felt the knell
In their belly & kept their mouth.
Better they'd left
Her memory as it was
Because the old girl they had walking around,
Hobbled far too close to obeah.

Dust

'...with the death of each old [woman] [my emphasis], a library is burnt'

Amadou Hampâté Bâ, Malian scholar

The weight of her words coil in the embers
Of a sky set-a-light over Kingston,
Her West-Indian epic remembers—
As breeze fans the thoughts of me her patron

Into flame. A library is burning.
And my face, dry with tears sees History
Committed to the soil, as i stand looking
On Spanish Oak. My genealogy

Is going, gone down with the griot whose
words were ample enough to contain.
Not big words; cut you up if they so choose,
No, words like a Djembe talking: the skin

Of language taut across a belly full
Of simple understanding, as ancient
As this thing between us, what would once fill
The breath words take, between the pregnant

Want of we: a language ourselves. Stories
That told of crippled boy-kings moving out
Of a beggars ignominy, or slaves,
Or a white-skinned great grandmother about

When slavery was as close as the night

26

After sundown, and it held the rawness
Of sweat under white cotton shirts, when white
Was held up against the 'Others' disgrace,

But with each day i know i'm forgetting,
Your photographs don't seem to move the heart,
Not in the same way. Either i'm healing
Or the burning of books have kept us apart.

Weightlifters' Belt

We were talking in her kitchen, two days after it
happened –
While he was in the kitchen
i stood at the door.
      As broad-backed as he was,
He had had the wind knocked out of him –
i could tell.
His words were tottering like a child's
And when we embraced,
i could feel him catching his breath
                    In the clinch.

My uncle bought a leather weightlifting belt
To carry his sick wife up and down two flights of
stairs
      'I did this every day for a year,' he said.
i imagine it was to support the lower lumbar
The base of his spinal column.
But now that he had removed the belt
               For good
Everything collapsed.
He was hunched over – had lifted to failure.
His arms slumped with the weight of it all,
His doughy frame, broken
Good for nothing.

And then i looked at his hair.
How he had become a wild man
Excavated to the ore,
His roots everywhere.

It was then i realised what had happened to him
He had given everything, all of his good everything
Just to see
His wife's spirit
Take up its bed
And walk.

Butterfly

Sunday, he went down into water dancing,
Between two ministers of the gospel
Whose black baptismal skirts hit the pool;
Changing state at the water surface.
His white shirt billowed like the crinoline
Of a jellyfish; the inner-man almost visible
Under the membrane of cotton
That swelled in the subtle undertow.
The water was troubled. And he danced
While his pallbearers stood either side.
When asked to say a few words,
He said to all witnesses present; that
He'd been through it. That before
He'd decided to put off the old-man, he was
Playing coy with Jesus. Besides, he had his lady,
And she was all the gospel he needed.
Then, she took sick. Doctor diagnosed right
After it had long had its way in her.
It almost turned him eunuch
For depression sake. Took him on a pilgrimage
To his first love. A love that ran him down,
Made him reason and say: *'here is water,
What does hinder me to be baptised.'* He wept.
Then with a raw rhythm of joy, man skanked
In some unseen celestial spotlight,
In his own dance hall before God.
And the ministers said, once he passes through
The water, he'd pass through the blood.
Put under in a plunge of bubbles
He went up from the water: his Father's womb,

Born again, with a righteous reggae outcry,
Steady rocking the bogle and the butterfly.

Pulpit Calypso

This title was put together based on an excerpt from the Introduction in The Oxford book of Caribbean verse 2005. The title 'Pulpit Calypso' intends to highlight a type of oral form that grew throughout the nineteenth century, after the abolition of slavery. Arguably, whether consciously or unconsciously the preachers of Jamaica and the West Indies may have linked the oral form of the sermon with the rhythmic and ludic quality that was found in Calypso —carrying with it: beauty, politics and Christian morality.

1948

I
At Tilbury fedoras funnel down
the gangplank and I did huddle there with
them a-grieve. Every man's an everyman,
the same age, a-hold-on-to little-faith.

Strangers, friends, faceless and packed like sardines
Stitched in their good suits, is some of the old
pulpit calypsonians in them teens:
Baptist preachers, Pentecostals, both bold

in themselves but flint-faced with the scripture,
moored now to the rock of *elsewhere*: this place
with its cold, over-sensitive weather
and cumulus that have water to waste.

I, answering the call for willing hands,
delivered phantom births that were waiting

in travail; once I arrived at the docks.—
It was the Wind, not Mother Land calling,

that same Spirit, the breath of God that put
my hands to labour in a place I knew
no more than Jamaica (my first love), but,
as I was a traveller passing through,

a servant who knew the weight of mandate
I feel 'pastor' was no suit to boast in,
but another way to communicate
my surrender within a second skin.

1958

II
So I'd blow music from the rostrum
of the pavements, to the dreadful pulpit
of the market square, armed with an old time
banner hymn, mic, amp, Caribbean lilt,

a gospel that danced crazy calypso,
making good news ecstatic with fever
yet not giddy to bend back like limbo
dancer, nor dead to lie down in slumber:

no, the preacher-man-tongue catch-a-fire,
until the sinner-man catch-a-fever
yes-soon the sinner-man catch-a-fire
till him ears-hard-heartbeat catch-a-fever.

My second set of eyes saw people born

in the spirit, how some sleep and wake
from a stupor that hit them harder than
life. — The afterlife doesn't really make

sense if we're a bag of bones, but, 'what if?'
Was the question asked in broken English,
(an English sized up, tailored for myself:
a cast net aimed at catching Men not fish.)

Patois, the Holy Spirit, tracts, pamphlets,
seemed enough to save even the Teddy
boy gangsters, still, these story from backstreets
made their way to the church testimony

service. — A Sister spoke of racism
at work, while singing two redemption songs
from the red book, a brother would spasm
mid-sentence of being saved from past wrongs.

Both, a part of a small congregation
in a little nook of Harlesden. A hall
littered with beer, blunts, bottles, that they'd clean
up the Sunday morning after Dancehall

Soca nights. —Brooms beardyman shuffled to
brush up the place making it look like church,
God was there with the people, the few,
it took two to have church, three for a march.

1960

III

Some called us a 'cult', or 'charismatic',
'The Black Church', a happy-clappy swinging
joint, like the Black Church in *Moby Dick*
where glossolalia would be tonguing

as flames in fits and starts. Otherworldly.
But aren't we all... Well, if you believe that
people are a lot older than how they
look, that this dirt-suit holds the infinite,

that God knew us before the very womb.
Then yes, otherworldly is what we were,
with a faith that de-fanged the very tomb,
denying the old life sucking vampire.

'O Death where is thy sting?' It's like He picked
up his two feet and left; the way they are
carrying on, as if there is no fixed
time, or date, that this life was not a war

we lose with the final blow of the breath.
        I was more than a seasoned preacher-man,
more than eyes to the body of a Faith
house in the navel of Brent. I was a man

above all else. Bringing small food baskets
to widows, lamenting with the mourners
long after tears turned to salt and caskets
were laid in the ground; sent off with prayers.

It says a lot that you should hear all that
after I'm gone. That these testimonies
should speak of me completely sold out
to a cause that fills me up and empties

me out. A love that can make a madman
out of anyone. Turning a father
into a preacher with a megaphone,
or a husband into a gospeller.

Cussin'

Since day
Cuss words volleyed
In arcs above the playground.
You cocked gun-fingers; would let go—
Trading tourettic rounds
Sputtering trigger-happy smut.
Those times, brothers were in love:
A few sparks to the face. A lacquered black-eye.
Rude-boy heart-broken,
Kissed hard on the mouth in a punch-up.
It's all love.

The gang
A storefront for poets
Had an emcees' bravado.
Wore screw-faces under *Avirex* leathers,
New eras over hoods in-a-hot-minute of English
summer.
You, *Say'dis*, *Killa* with an *a*,
Used the blade-end of words
On playground turned pirate radio emcees.
Blood, an emcee got slewed back in the day,
Stripped of the alias, but brother walked away
With his life.

Your tongue
Did twang and take set back then.
Now brothers get gunned down to nothing. For
nothing.
A smudge on white Nike Air Force Ones.

Gunned down to another gully bed in a cemetery.
Another brother caught slipping
In-between postcodes on his jack jones,
Left punctured, drained, until he slept away.
Your crew played like TV Indian and Cowboys,
Compared to those that can't even dignify
A brother with the indignity
Of a cuss.

Graffiti

Sprawling
the Metropolitan line
walking the walls till they overrun,
and that which litter the walls loiter
between breaths of daylight;
on the ride from
Wembley Park to Baker Street

here words are meeting
having it out,
going at it out-
side the lines,
breaking English with Englishes,

cutting its teeth
on the knife-edge
of local lingua-franca,
turning-out words that join
then splinter into skirmishes

of wildstyle inciting
riot, stirring quiet anarchy.
scrawling script, stark and streaking,
infinitely winds into meaningful meaning.
To each wall - a madness,

to each wall its own rant.

Catching Brent

At this spot: the station at North Wembley.
Above the flash of train tracks, faded Graff,
Trains whipping like schitz electricity;
You can see the borough sunning itself.

The clichés of Wembley for the moment
Are upheld and poetry is captured
With a blackbird cotched on a satellite
Dish. Birds, maybe magpies silhouetted

And stippled against the white-balanced sky
Tightrope on the aerials on chimneys
Trembling the wiry limbs before they fly.
Look down toward rolling roads, where the trees

Lined out like commas, list buildings along
East Lane. Semi-detached houses, shops,
The roads ribboning between the shale; sling
The vehicles on these highlighted roads.

The concrete, the soil, balances the scene,
And this teetering in-between of the
Man-made and that which has come to mean
More, is that which words struggle to measure.

Mister Nobody

Always at a sideways lean

Suited in pavement herringbone,

Eclipse of a Black man

Cast-down – as the ellipse

Behind the word 'Negro,'

Those long shadows behind words

(Yawning in their history books)

Are haunted for true.

But this Mister Nobody,

Refuses to live like murder.

Instead, He roots himself to

Transients, walking Baobabs,

Upside-down men, women

With races roiling,

Sensibilities becoming,

Tongues flailing and soul-tied,

Those diluted Negroes

Who know shade is as night

Passing— the fettered

To someplace

Elsewhere.

Box man

Paralysis of the hearts sense of direction is the box man's chronic complaint.

Kobo Abe, *Box Man*

his life
like past lives
like hand-me-downs
baggy, borrowed
      wears heavy
in his blood;
heavy on his mind

with guilt
he occupies
this life of which
used to be theirs,
      they've gone on
but it's their expectation
occupies him,

his skin
was theirs also,
its fashion no choice of his own
just some old clothes
      that wears him,
and wants to be worn
the way it must,

with pride,
not kept to corners,

yet this suit
can be a box
      to a heart
that like a waving white flag,
flies for no country,

his heart,
yielding to the breath
of a life in the lung of destiny,
knows no such sojourn,
      and longs to drift
back out on the current
that took him to this island, this body—

with need,
his ageless soul,
his sexless spirit,
finds its sail in
      love everlasting,
its bearings in the expanse
of that limitless sea.

Reggae (island longing)

He frets that guitar.
Frets the strum to shimmering,
Sets the metronome

To wearing bare feet
Like shoes, so that mind and mind
Can walk together

Colour blind. Reggae:
The sound of life limping cool,
Passed yard men drowning

Red evenings in Red
Stripe Beer. Running ambitious
Men into the night

With steel pans, smoked meats,
To season the sky with Scotch
Bonnet and Jerk Spice.

The pulse of reggae
Is seen in the shallow lust
Of the mosquito,

The night agitates—
Man nor woman will stay one
Place. And at the beach

Edge, where cicadas

Click, blinkies* catch light, alight
And then short circuit—

The sea is going,
Going on steady rising
And falls to a low

Island heat, taming
At room temperature in
This Caribbean.

This is living life.
Listening to him playing
Is like living life.

Still, the rocking of
His song can only idle
This island longing.

One Jamaica Morning

In from the sea
A drawn-out breath blows
Through Island yard
Clothes: Airing the
Damp Palm fronds,
Full slips and half slips
Of the Acacias,
And fingers through the
Breadfruit leaves' tasselled
Overhang, drip-drying all
Touched by the little dew; (as
Jamaica don't rain like England).
The same wind
Troubles the ackee
In their topmost canopies
Stirring the morning
Out of sleep.

***

Today, i beat the cockerel
To the sun.
He clears his throat
Long after i stalk road
And bound beach
To catch day
Unawares.
To watch as tourist watch
(But not quite)
The sea work like any

47

Knotty dread artist
In down town Kingston.
Chopping at deadwood
To refine fetish for
Foreigner and
Foreign mantel pieces:
Images of the Dr. Bird, lignum vitae or
Some fertility god
Then watch him blow dust
From behind the
Jutting when he's done
And feel it on my face
Like sand blowing in
From the sea.

***

10:00 am. Auntie hails a taxi-
man. i speak in nods.
He can see through it,
My gestures sound
Nothing like patois.
So I smile easy, my smile say, 'i
Understand, but don't speak.'
          'We a go a town,' Auntie say.
She's my interpreter.
i turn away, taking in the road, the
Potholes, zinc houses, plazas
As town creeps
Up on rural Jamaica.
Houses seem to have grown
Out of the soil,
Trees lean on the shoulders

Of zinc shacks sponsored
By Digicel and Lime.

Both bank and road are
Comfortable in one-anothers space
Rubble blends into sand and
Rockstone
Doting on each other
As old friends. Making good
Of an old truce, an
Old forgotten spat between
God and Man.
The land and road roll together
In a giddy whoosh,
Jamaica is a hairy-skinned girl
The road her husband.
Everywhere
She greens—
Shocking pink
Bougainvilleas come up
On her skin
Puckered like hickeys.
Boy, Jamaica!
She seem well ripe to be
Picked. Well ripe and ready,
With such ferocious fecundity
That the very mountainside
Exposes a little flesh.
But it's the kernel
i want, it's the boiling passions
Of the heart; I want.

The real heart,
The one found in the belly…
So i will use this poetry
As a stone, beating the white of
The almond morning for fruit.

***

'Driver! The drive sweet ee man',
Auntie say,
'We a go market, so likkle more!'

We step out on Kingston.
She, navigating the stalls
Me with camera 'a pop style'
Like tourist.
'Mek sure yu a follow close *close*.'

The eyes of the *higglers*
Can smell the foreigner in my walk,
Can sense my loose
Understanding of Jamaican
Dollars. How me Black 'English
Man', look on the face of Sir Donald Sangster,
Norman Manley, and see only money.
Roadside is lined with
Sellers, the old and the young
Are possessed with an ole
Entrepreneurial Spirit
As they are with the old religion and
Reggae. Down to the infants recite
A barters' refrain – natural dub poets

Called out of necessity.
The foreign and occasional scent
Of American pop riffs are barely
Heard over the pulse of the road's
Hungry belly.
Buy. Sell. Haggle. Settle. Move...
Move...
Boy, the culture's skin's tough
Rendering the Other
To sugar cane trash.

　　　"Nice Orange, ripe orange! O-R-A-N-G-E."
Bursts from this plump mommy
In Rastaman chants.
Her long calico dress dips
As she stoops and straddles her
Wicker basket.

***

All this time
The sun comes off the asphalt,
Thaws the road into
Rivers.
The dry banks crack with lizards.
Trees crack their bones.
Again the day yawns.

Zinc fence shadows take noonday siestas.
PNP is scrawled angry on stone government buildings
And boarded-up shop fronts,
(Old business is moved to New

Kingston).

***

A street dog passes
Pregnant with wind,
His maw sweating over
Spread out trench,
Some old colonial latrine
Left to stagnate in the
Market middle

***

'Jamaica nutt'n but money, politics and obeah sah!'
One man says to his friend.

i tread my aunt's shadow
And listen wide to
Snatch volleys of
Market Creole.
Crab women brood
Over dasheen mounds,
Placing the fattest
Yellow yams at the top
To hide the meagre tubers.
Other sellers pitch beds
Next to their mounds,
Some speak bad mind on their
Neighbours gift offerings.
i tell you Coronation market
Can make man crazy like mad ants.
i just see a man swear he would
Step on this woman's head,

It must be the blood of the Maroon
Or the Abeng in her voice,
Because she shattered his spirit
Good good like 'Mosquito' Indian.—

Auntie's bag full till *him* want throw up,
The flimsy black scandal bottom
Is tearing out; as if to make
A show of our earnings.
i watch Auntie struggle in the sun.
Her red skin bleeds.
Sun hot man.
          'Auntie, let me carry the bag,' i say.
          'Boy, Jamaica hard but it good bad,' she say.

          'Jamaica hard, but it good bad.'
i smile at this, smile at the day in fact.
Then a tear betrays me

i don't worry myself, is just my mind
Sharing a joke with itself
My belly playing tricks,
But I can't say the joke back again

My belly knows,
It knows exactly
How my soul
Wants to be

And the joke is:
i can't say what that is.

In the cool of its shade

'And the leaves of the tree were for the healing of the nations.'
Revelation 22:2

Outside *Bay Church* window, church is going
On. From this pew of birch i sit thinking

There's no difference, but for the preachers.—
The outdoor preacher with its palm fingers,

With a breeze like Spirit shot up in its
Bones; its backlit leaves in slow-rocking praise

Stands unfazed by the others religion.
       i watched how it leaned to wicker the sun

And how easy the sunlight made shadows
Squat and sit to dying shade. Change happens

In subtle beams; feathering the green skull
Cap of the yard, on plants round the root— all

Spoke without a word. This leafy parson
Had a way with silences, its sermon;

i'll call it that, wasn't a preachy one,
The message rang out in light on blanched stone

And warmth, that comes from holding it in your
Hands, something firm, like faith held together

In palms of fervent prayer. That feeling
Rests in the play of light, in the shifting

Chiaroscuro, and moves with the mood
Of the afternoon. And this preacher had

An ordinary commonplace that made
Me feel footsteps in the cool of its shade.

Elephant dance

Even now i dig wells.
And speak to situations
With warbling footsteps.

i draw water and blood from
Deep welts of promise, and
Stomp up a steady thunderhead.

With legs like tree trunks
Mouth like bugle, i march.
i change the atmosphere,

Break fallow ungiving
Circumstance, those
Moments; set-in-their-ways,

Stubborn as dead men
Stubborn as cemeteries.
But i keep stamping.

Water is near, i hear it
Riding the incus,
Galloping in the turning dust

i keep stamping.
Like a shadow that echoes
The call-back of the sun

i keep stamping.

To drown out the echo of
Unbelief.

i keep stamping.

i keep stamping

Until water comes.

Coming to Come

We,
Coming to come
Are readying
The same way night
Is becoming-morning
We,
Tomorrow's children
Wade horizons
Dusting off
Yesterday's thresholds
After every
Crossing
We,
Transitioning
Are ourselves
A seamless changing
As forever rides us
As conscience
We,
Dying daily
Are edifying
Winds within bones
Spirited houses
Of faith
And flesh
Moving
We,
Coming
And going
Are the greatest

Event hurtling
Through a string of
Present-future-pasts

Lightning Source UK Ltd.
Milton Keynes UK
UKOW04f0700241215

265231UK00002B/10/P